D1209713

365
TABLE GRACES
FOR THE
CHRISTIAN HOME

Charles L. Wallis

365

TABLE GRACES

FOR THE

CHRISTIAN HOME

Harper & Row, Publishers
New York, Evanston, and London

First Edition

Library of Congress Catalog Card Number: 67-14939
Designed by The Etheredges

Inscribed to
EARL W. BENJAMIN

CONTENTS

TABLE GRACES
FOR
FIFTY-TWO
WEEKS

FIRST WEEK

Sunday

Lord of the Sabbath, stand no longer at the door of our home, but come and sup with us and we with thee, for by thy coming our lives are blessed, our love is deepened, and this day is made radiant by thy presence. We pray that at home and in church today we may be given such spiritual strength and fortitude as may be essential for all of the requirements of the days of this week.

Monday

As the scattered grains of the field have been gathered into a single loaf of bread, so are we drawn together, dear Lord, from our many occupations and activities into one family fellowship with thee.

Tuesday

Help us, dear loving God, not to forget thy benefits toward us, for they are beyond our deserving and greater than any claim we may justly make of thy divine providence.

Wednesday

Dear God, who didst create the first family and didst ordain that every man should know the blessings of loved ones, create within our hearts a love for all of thy children.

Thursday
We praise and thank thee, dear God, for thou dost feed the whole world, not only with that which gives strength to our bodies, but also with thy goodness, loving-kindness, and tender mercies for the strengthening of our souls.

Friday
Heavenly Father, bless us and keep us, make thy face to shine upon us, and be gracious unto us, both now while we eat together and also when we resume our various chores and activities.

Saturday
Help each of us to dedicate his differing talents to the up-building of our family ties, for we know, dear Lord, that the blessings of this home will support all of our experiences and endeavors.

SECOND WEEK

Sunday

Dear Jesus, who didst feed the multitude with five barley loaves and two small fishes offered by one small lad, may we on this holy Sabbath feel close to our brethren in every land who bow their heads in prayer and lift their voices in songs of praise, and may we willingly and gladly set aside a portion of what is ours for the feeding of thy hungry children wherever they may live.

Monday

We thank thee, Lord of heaven and earth, for this food taken from the soil of the land and the waters of the sea, and for its preparation for our use by tender and loving hands.

Tuesday

We, who cannot know by name the many people who in one way or another have shared in growing, harvesting, and preparing this food, offer to thee, O God, our joyous thanksgiving for all persons who labor for our health and happiness.

Wednesday

Dear Jesus, who didst bless the bread and give it to thy

4

disciples in the Upper Room in Jerusalem, bless this bread for our use and us to thy service.

Thursday

For the abundance of spiritual and material blessings which thou hast given to us, dear God, we offer thee our humble and sincere thanksgiving, and we pray that these blessings may bring health to our bodies and cheerfulness to our lives.

Friday

We remember, dear Christ, the promise of thy presence where two or three are gathered together in thy name, and we ask thee to be with us as we partake of this food in thy name.

Saturday

Even as the sun by day and the lamp by night bring light to this room and family table, so may thy Son become for us not only the Light of the world but also a light within us.

THIRD WEEK

Sunday

On this day which thou, O God, hast made, we would rejoice and be glad in it. We thank thee for the health of our bodies. May we eat this meal in perfect confidence, peace, and trust.

Monday

These foods, now set before us, are symbols of thy loving-kindness, dear heavenly Father, and each dish reminds us of thy providential care and of thy wish that we should eat in joy and contentment.

Tuesday

We accept this food and thy many blessings in thankfulness, dear God, knowing that nothing we have done or said makes us worthy, but knowing that thou dost nonetheless love us and that thou hast claimed us for thyself.

Wednesday

While seated at this our family table, we cherish the blessed memories of those whose chairs are empty and who are now at thy right hand at the heavenly table which thou hast prepared in thy house of many mansions.

Thursday

May the peace of God, which passeth all understanding, enter into our hearts during this meal, and teach us to nurture harmony and happiness in our beloved home.

Friday

Dear Christ, who art the Bread of life, feed our souls with thy love so that we may be nourished both in body and in soul.

Saturday

We wish to dwell, dear Lord, in the secret place of the Most High and to abide under the shadow of the Almighty, not only as we eat this meal in thankfulness, but also as we pursue our work and responsibilities during the daylight hours and as we rest during the night.

FOURTH WEEK

Sunday

From the busy pressures of the week's routines we have come together on this thy day, dear heavenly Father, to share the joy of our family circle and to offer to thee our thanksgiving for food, home, and this fellowship of love.

Monday

We thank thee, loving Father, that thou didst create day and night, seedtime and harvest, and this food which we accept in thy name. We pray that we may ever grow into thy likeness and according to thy divine will.

Tuesday

Help us, gracious God, always to think of our bodies as temples wherein thy Holy Spirit dwells, and may we always make room for thy Spirit to work through our lives.

Wednesday

So discipline in love our hands and feet, our minds and thoughts, our words and actions, dear God, that at this table and away we may think thy thoughts, do thy work, and glorify thy holy name.

8

Thursday

We thank thee, our Father, for the farms, factories, and markets from which has come this food for our enjoyment and nourishment, and we pray that we may be grateful for the labors of all who have provided for our needs.

Friday

O thou who didst so love the world that thou didst give for us thy only begotten Son, teach us so to love one another, both those at this table and also thy children everywhere, that our lives may mirror thy great and abiding love.

Saturday

Dear Christ, who art our silent Guest at this and every meal, be with us as we partake of this food, may our conversation honor thee, and may our fellowship glorify thee.

FIFTH WEEK

Sunday

Our God, who hath breathed into our lungs the breath of thy life and strengthened us for every worthy and useful task, as we sit at this table we pray that the words of our mouths and the meditations of our hearts be acceptable to thee. Bless, we pray thee, all who this day proclaim thy Word in sermons and lessons and all who proclaim thy love through deeds of loving-kindness.

Monday

We thank thee, O Lord, that thy good gifts of sun and rain and fertile soil have brought from tiny seeds the bountiful harvest of vegetables and fruits here provided by thy love for the strengthening of our bodies.

Tuesday

Bless and protect our loved ones, wherever they may be, dear God, and give to them and us the desire and will to do whatever may be required for the upbuilding of thy kingdom.

Wednesday

Help us to learn, dear Lord, that peace and brotherhood will come to this world only as men permit a loving spirit to control their hearts and to govern their relations with those with whom they eat their daily bread.

Thursday

We thank thee, our Father, for those who labor to bring food to our table and all who grow the food which offers delight to our tongues and health to our bodies.

Friday

We acknowledge, dear Lord, thy ownership and our stewardship of all that is contained within this world, and we pray that we may so harvest the fruits of the fields that no man may be deprived of the food needed for his health and happiness.

Saturday

Although food is placed before us day by day and year after year, may we not, merciful Father, take the preparation of these good things for granted but rather continually call to remembrance in gratefulness the loving hands which cook and serve.

SIXTH WEEK

Sunday

Dear God, who hast placed us in this wonderful world and given to us the first day of each week for praise, reflection, and meditation, open wide our eyes that we may truly see the beauties of field and forest and so come at last to a greater and more sensitive appreciation of the miracles of bread and meat.

Monday

Guide us, dear Lord, throughout this day. Help us cheerfully to accept thy will and obediently to follow thy commandments. May this food bring health to our bodies and thy Word bring renewal of strength to our souls.

Tuesday

At this table, heavenly Father, our cups of happiness overflow, not only because of thy generous provision of food and drink, but also because we sit with those who love us and those whom we love in thy name.

Wednesday

Dear God, as we eat this good food, now prepared for our use, may thy great love become very real to us, and may we partake in the certain knowledge that thou wilt show us how we may more perfectly love one another.

Thursday

For bread which strengthens our hearts, for drink which refreshens our spirits, and for thy companionship with us at this table, we offer our joyous thanksgiving.

Friday

Dear God, may we in love preferring one another consider the needs of other persons before we seek to satisfy only the hunger of our own bodies and the cravings of our own hearts.

Saturday

Not by this bread only do we live, holy Father, but by every good and precious word which comes to us from thee are we made strong to live full and triumphant lives.

SEVENTH WEEK

Sunday

Heavenly Father, who didst raise thy Son Jesus Christ with power from death and the grave and hast given us one day in seven wherein especially to proclaim his living presence through worship and testimony, may we welcome him to a place with us at this table and feel his power within us as we look forward to the responsibilities of this new week.

Monday

We thank thee, dear Lord, not merely that we have board and room, but that by thy grace we also have each other and this food which we most enjoy when we are permitted to share it together at this table.

Tuesday

Dear God, whose Spirit has borne witness with our spirits that we are thy children, may we live as thy obedient children, accepting thy fatherly love with open hearts and breaking this bread ever in gratitude to thee.

Wednesday

Help us, our Father, to eat this food reverently and never to waste that which might give health to a hungry child, and may we not want more than we truly need in a world where so many would gladly accept crumbs from our table.

Thursday

If we face challenges today for which we are not prepared and if we must undertake responsibilities which are too heavy, make thy power, heavenly Father, available and give us thy guidance.

Friday

Relieve our hearts from the burden of regret for yesterday's sins, dear Lord, and by thy forgiveness renew our spirits within us, and may we eat this food in cheerfulness and serve thee in faithfulness.

Saturday

O thou who art the way, the truth, and the life, we pray that thou wilt show us thy way, reveal to us thy truth, and open before us thy radiant life so that at this table fellowship with our loved ones we may come to know new spiritual breadth and height and depth.

EIGHTH WEEK

Sunday

Dear Jesus, thou hast called us to go into all the world to preach thy gospel. We pray that thy Holy Spirit may inspire all preachers, missionaries, and teachers who this day interpret thy holy Word. And bless our words also, so we may do and say what is pleasing unto thee.

Monday

May we who are seated at this table which shows our common love and concern feel so close to thee that we shall never consider the doing of thy will to be a burden but rather a privilege and a delight.

Tuesday

Dear Christ, we pause in the midst of a day crowded with duties and activities to center our thoughts on thee and thankfully to acknowledge thy many gifts. May this moment of family prayer remind us that a life centered in thee will have purpose and balance.

Wednesday

Dear God of love, may we rise in the morning with hearts filled with love, may we sit at this table with hearts filled with love, may we turn to our activities, whether in work or recreation, with hearts filled with love, and may we retire for the night with hearts renewed with love.

Thursday

Dear God, who didst lead thy children through the wilderness with a cloud by day and a flame by night and didst feed them with a heavenly manna, lead us, too, we pray thee, and bring us again to this table according to thy mercies and for thy name's sake.

Friday

O thou who hast given to each of us different talents, we pray that we may each do so well the work which thou hast given us that the Master shall say, "Well done, good and faithful servant."

Saturday

Give us during life's darkest days a song in our hearts so that we may ever sit at this table in the confident trust that thou dost desire thy children to be cheerful.

17

NINTH WEEK

Sunday

On this day of quiet and peace, when we are permitted to refrain from the obligations of daily labor, we ask thee, dear Lord, especially to bless all those who work while we sleep and toil while we rest, and bless all farmers, merchants, and deliverymen who make it possible each day for us to have a table provided with food and strength for our bodies.

Monday

O God, may it not be necessary for us to be deprived of food before we learn to be thankful for thy daily provision, but may we always be mindful that these common gifts are an evidence of thy uncommon love.

Tuesday

Cleanse the thoughts of our minds by the inspiration of thy Holy Spirit, dear God, so we may gratefully receive and worthily partake of this food which has been prepared for the strengthening of our bodies.

Wednesday

Heavenly Father, even as we season this food so the taste may be delightful, so season our lives with thy grace and

love that we may bring cheerfulness and hope to all whose
lives touch ours.

Thursday

Dear God, who hast made us in thy image and hast
called us thy children, may our lives become holy temples
in which thy Spirit dwells, and may we always, both at
this table and away, do those things which honor and
glorify thee.

Friday

May our central purpose both at this table and throughout
this day be none other than to restore the spirit of the
living Christ in our home and in our lives.

Saturday

Dear God, bless this nation and state, our president and
governor, all elected and appointed officials, and all others
who contribute to our peace and security.

TENTH WEEK

Sunday

We break this bread here at our table, almighty God, even as we share in the breaking of bread with fellow Christians in our various places of worship this day, in the certain knowledge that we partake of the life and work of our Lord Jesus Christ.

Monday

Teach us, dear Lord, good table manners both in regard to the manner in which we eat this food which thou hast prepared for us and with respect to the way we speak to our loved ones whom thou hast given to be our closest companions.

Tuesday

Dear God, may this food give us sufficient strength so that we may do our part in the world's work.

Wednesday

Heavenly Father, may our family fellowship ever inspire us to godly living. As we eat this food, may we speak only kind and encouraging words. Help us always to remember our Lord and Master and faithfully to follow him.

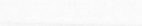

Thursday

Quicken in us, O God, a lively sense of gratitude to thee for all of thy good gifts: a roof above our heads, a family drawn together in love, and this food for the nourishment of our bodies.

Friday

Dear God, may we, according to thy command, cast our bread upon the waters, knowing that more than enough for our need will return to us, and may we, according to thy requirement, share what we have with others, knowing that our giving is in obedience to thy holy will.

Saturday

May these few moments of prayer, dear Father, shut out the noises of the world so that we may in peace enjoy this goodly fellowship of our family circle.

ELEVENTH WEEK

Sunday

Dear Christ, even as thou didst make thyself known in the home at Emmaus in the breaking of bread, so may we come to know thee more perfectly as we share this loaf which thou hast provided for our need. May this Lord's Day be a blessing in our lives, and may our lives bless thee this week.

Monday

Because our table is spread with such an abundance of good food and the tables of so many of thy precious children have little or no food, help us to recall our Master's words that whatsoever we do for any unfortunate brother we do for thee and in thy name.

Tuesday

Dear God, who maketh us to lie down in green pastures and leadeth us beside still waters, thou hast prepared this table for our joy and nourishment, and to thee we offer the thanksgiving of our hearts.

Wednesday

May our lives, strengthened by this food, truly become a living sacrifice, holy, acceptable unto thee and dedicated to serving one another and all who are within thy worldwide kingdom.

Thursday

Dear God, who hast taught us that when we draw nigh to thee, thou wilt draw nigh to us, may we make a place at this table and within our hearts for thy presence.

Friday

We offer our thanks to thee, heavenly Father, for thy ineffable gifts of house and home, food and drink, health and happiness, and especially for the living presence of thy Son Jesus Christ.

Saturday

Dear Jesus Christ, who art the Lord of our lives and the Master of our minds and hearts, we pray that thou wilt be the Host at this our family table.

TWELFTH WEEK

Sunday

Dear Jesus Christ, who art the same, yesterday, today, and forever, bring into our lives on this Lord's Day a knowledge that thou art always near and keep us true in our devotion and steadfastly loyal to thee and thy kingdom.

Monday

Dear Father, may the spiritual climate of this home nurture and encourage the growth of every Christian grace and beauty.

Tuesday

Support us, eternal Father, with thy everlasting arms so that all we do and say at this table and abroad in the world may be a witness of our trust in thy love and protection.

Wednesday

Give us grace, dear Jesus, at this time to accept penitently this food set before us, to take up daily whatever cross of loving and sacrificial service thou dost give us, and faithfully to follow wherever thou dost lead us.

24

Thursday

Help us to remember, dear God, that our expressions of thankfulness, however ardent and sincere, are insufficient if we do not do justly, love mercy, and walk humbly with thee.

Friday

Dear God, may the spirit of Christ be as evident in this house as the sunshine at the window, the fresh air at the door, and the food upon our table.

Saturday

Dear Jesus Christ, we know that thou art a teacher come from God, and we earnestly pray that we may be ready pupils in thy school of life, learning always to give thee thanks when we eat and to serve thee faithfully in our work and recreation.

THIRTEENTH WEEK

Sunday

Dear God, we recall the precious memory of our loved ones who in other years gathered with us about this table and worshiped with us in church and have given to us inspiring examples of noble Christian living, and we pray that one day we may be found deserving through thy sacrificial love to be gathered with them and thee in thy blessed home beyond the Jordan.

Monday

May our family devotions and prayers daily inspire us to do thy will, O God, even as thy Son Jesus found in his small home in Nazareth the inspiration and guidance to undertake thy holy work.

Tuesday

Thy breath, dear Lord, hath given us life, and from thy storehouse have come these treasures of food and drink. May our lips forever praise thee and our lives forever serve thee.

Wednesday

Dear God, who didst create this world and all that is therein, we thank thee for thy love which is manifested in

26

sun and shower, in soil and seed, and in the ripened fruit and grain given to us for daily food.

Thursday

May our home be founded, heavenly Father, upon him who is the Rock of true faith and not upon the shifting sands of doubt, and may we accept this food with prayerful thanksgiving and not with spiritual apathy.

Friday

Dear Jesus, who didst lay down thy life for thy friends, may we follow thy example and give of our time and strength in love to those with whom we share this meal and this home.

Saturday

Great Physician, bless all who suffer and are afflicted, use us in thy healing ministry, and grant us patience and hope in our own times of difficulty.

FOURTEENTH WEEK

Sunday

Dear Jesus Christ, whose first churches were the houses of thy faithful disciples, may our beloved home be made holy by our prayers and our loving service to one another and to thee. Even as thy church gives strength to our home, so may we take into our church the love and loyalty to thee which we have found in our family.

Monday

May we, dear God, express our thankfulness for this food by cheerfully doing whatever thou dost require and loyally following thy guidance.

Tuesday

We thank thee, our Father, for the beauty of this earth, for the security of this nation, for the love of this family, and for this food which we now eat in thy name.

Wednesday

Make this table, heavenly Father, a family altar at which we offer the sacrifices of joyful and grateful hearts for the abundance of good food which thou hast provided for our nourishment.

Thursday

Dear Lord and Master, come and share with us the breaking of bread and the fellowship of this meal, and may thy spirit be present at this table and in our hearts.

Friday

Kindle within our hearts, merciful Spirit, the flame of gratitude for this food, this warm house, our loved ones, and the privilege of living in thy great and beautiful world.

Saturday

May this food, dear God, give us strength, and then renewed in body and spirit, may we use this strength to serve thee by our words, our work, and our example of fidelity and loyalty to thee.

FIFTEENTH WEEK

Sunday

Enlarge, dear God, the circumference of our family circle to include our neighborhood, our community, our nation, and the family of all mankind. Bless all who seek this day to broaden the horizons of Christian love. May thy benediction rest upon all pastors and congregations, all Sunday school teachers and pupils, all missionaries and those to whom are introduced and interpreted thy wonderful words of life.

Monday

From the rising of the sun this day unto the going down of the same, may thy holy name, O God, be praised, for thou hast provided for the necessities of our bodies and given light to our souls.

Tuesday

O thou who art gracious and merciful, slow to anger and of great kindness, accept the thanksgiving of thy children, and may we eat this food in the assurance that thou dost ever love us.

Wednesday

Dear Lord Jesus, who didst teach us that it is more blessed

to give than to receive, may we accept thy gift of food
with thankfulness and dedicate our strengthened bodies
to thee and to our fellow men.

Thursday

We pray, dear Lord, that we may ever be kind and con-
siderate to one to another in brotherly love, both as we eat
this meal and when we turn to the work and play of
family living.

Friday

May this ordinary meal become extraordinarily meaning-
ful through the gaining by us of some new insight from
thy Holy Word and some new appreciation for the personalities of those with whom we now eat this food.

Saturday

May thy blessings descend like the gentle rains of heaven
upon the lives of all who sit at this table, bringing peace,
joy, and an ardent desire to fulfill thy divine purposes
in our lives.

SIXTEENTH WEEK

Sunday

We thank thee, dear God, that of old thou didst ordain that this shall be a day of rest for our bodies and for the uplifting of our souls. May we dedicate a portion of the sunlight hours to holy thoughts and activities, and may we at sundown so seek for thee in prayer and meditation that we shall be enabled this week to live as worthy heirs of thy kingdom.

Monday

Dear Lord and Savior, who art near us from infancy even to old age, bless this home. May we not only share this meal in concord and cheerfulness but also grow together in every Christian virtue.

Tuesday

We who are members of one household have individual needs, gracious Father, and we pray that in some private manner thou wilt minister to the particular desires of each of us at this family table.

Wednesday

As we lift our heads to drink from these cups, dear God, may we also lift our hearts in praise to thee and raise our eyes to behold the wondrous world which thou hast prepared to be our home.

Thursday

Dear Father in heaven, we thank thee for clean water and for pure food, and we acknowledge our indebtedness to all upon whom rests the responsibility for making certain that this food and drink give health to our bodies.

Friday

Make thou thy home at our table and in our lives, dear Jesus, so that we may have thy peace within our herats.

Saturday

Help us, merciful Savior, to understand that no food, however good and tasty, will satisfy our inner need if we do not quench our thirst at the true fountain of all spiritual living, which is the Holy Spirit.

SEVENTEENTH WEEK

Sunday
Give us some worthwhile task to do for thy glory, dear God, and the ability to do it worthily. Give us the spirit of sincere gratitude for all who, having done conscientiously their work, have provided the food on this table. Give us also the quiet satisfaction which comes with the knowledge that we have done our best.

Monday
Dear Lord, fill our hearts with thankfulness and our souls with love for thee and for each other.

Tuesday
Help us, heavenly Father, to accept the pleasures of this day in gratitude, the sorrows of this day in patience, and the responsibilities of this day in faithfulness.

Wednesday
Blessed God and Father, may we in heartfelt gratitude remember all toil-worn hands that till the soil, all skillful hands that harvest, all loving hands that cook and serve, and thy hand which rests upon us all.

Thursday

Make us ever conscious, dear Lord, that our chief purpose is to serve and love thee in whatever we do, whether in eating, working, playing, or resting.

Friday

Dear God, teach us that as thou hast given this food to us, so we, too, are expected to share whatever we possess with any whose need is greater than our own.

Saturday

Blessed Savior, who long ago in Galilee didst turn water into wine, we thank thee for the miraculous manner by which thou dost transform the food on this table into new strength and energy within our bodies.

EIGHTEENTH WEEK

Sunday

Keep bright and clean the windows of heaven, gracious God, so we may always be able to look upon thy throne and ever remember the many ways thy love has blessed us. Open our hearts this day to the ministry of thy Word in church worship, and increase our faith as we thy servants partake gratefully of this food which is a silent witness of thy providential concern for us.

Monday

We who are young and we who are old have with the Psalmist of Israel never seen thy righteous people forsaken nor their children begging bread. For this and thy innumerable blessings, we praise and thank thy holy name.

Tuesday

May this family table and our home be such a spiritual lighthouse, dear Lord, that not only shall we be guided aright in all we do but all others may find here the light of thy love.

Wednesday

Because our hearts are restless until they find rest in thee,

our heavenly Father, renew once more our vision of thee
and give us thy peace as we eat this meal.

Thursday

Merciful and loving God, give us such compassion and
sympathy for the needs of others that we shall not wish
to eat food at our table without first praying for our less
fortunate fellow men.

Friday

We thank thee, O holy and ever-blessed Lord, for our sense
of hunger, not merely for that which satisfies our physical
cravings, but even more for thy Holy Word which satisfies
our spiritual longings.

Saturday

Eternal God, who knowest our need before we ask and
art ever willing to supply our wants according to thy
riches in glory, keep us keenly aware of thy providential
love while we share in the bounties of this table and when
we are called to walk in the paths of work and duty.

NINETEENTH WEEK

Sunday

O God of love, bless the missionaries of thy church wherever they live and labor on this Sabbath. May our prayers for them and theirs for us forge links binding their tables and their professions of faith to ours. If they are lonely and weary, comfort them, dear God, and keep them steadfast in their calling, even as we pray that thou wilt keep us steadfast in the work thou hast assigned to us.

Monday

Abide with us, Lord Jesus, inspire our souls, animate our conversations, encourage our love for one another, and bless this food that it may truly become a means whereby we may more worthily achieve citizenship within thy kingdom.

Tuesday

We thank and bless thee, heavenly Father, for our family now gathered about this table, and we ask thee to bless all whom we love and all families everywhere who are our brothers in thee.

Wednesday

Dear Father, keep us from the temptation of taking for

granted and without thankfulness the three meals provided each day, and may each meal become an opportunity to renew our appreciation of thy divine love.

Thursday

May this food, dear God, restore the strength of our bodies so that we may serve thee and our fellow men today through hard and honest work.

Friday

God of love, we who become so easily angered and irritated when we cannot have our own way seek more earnestly to know thy will and to do it, for only by a sincere and heartfelt commitment shall we be enabled to eat this bread in peace and joy.

Saturday

Lord Jesus, we pray that thou who art the Word made flesh may dwell with us today. Give us bread for our bodies and thy living presence for our souls.

TWENTIETH WEEK

Sunday

Dear Jesus, who hast taught us that when we ask, thou wilt give to us the desires of our hearts, and when we seek, thou wilt show us the way, and when we knock, thou wilt open for us the doors of life, we thy children do now ask, seek, and knock in the knowledge that thou wilt bless this meal with thy presence and this day of rest with thy abiding spirit.

Monday

Dear God, may we in the spirit of Christian kindness seek not so much to be served as to serve others and desire not so much to claim this good food for ourselves as to share it with those in our family.

Tuesday

May our home, O God, truly become a house of prayer and a temple of thy Spirit. May thou grant us to break bread together in love and trust and kindness.

Wednesday

Thy showers of blessing, heavenly Father, have turned small seeds into the good food placed before us and have transformed the dull routines of our common days into opportunities to serve thee with enthusiasm and zest.

Thursday

Dear compassionate Father, we who seldom go to bed hungry offer in love this prayer for thy children who seldom have enough to eat. Do not permit us to forget or neglect those who are less fortunate than we.

Friday

Thy greatest gift to us, dear God, is eternal life through Christ our Lord in whose name we do now eat this food and to whom we dedicate this day.

Saturday

Merciful Savior, cleanse our spirit and renew us on this last day of the week, that we may be more perfectly prepared to worship thee tomorrow and to accept the privileges and joys which the new week may bring.

TWENTY-FIRST WEEK

Sunday

Because thy loving-kindness is better than life, dear God, our lips shall praise thee this day within thy temple and during this hour of joyous companionship at this meal. Make bright and radiant our faith in thee so that we shall feel thee near us when we take up this week the responsibilities of school and office and factory.

Monday

Give us, dear Lord, an appetite not only for the savory food now set before us, but also for all good and worthy thoughts which thou dost communicate to us by thy Holy Spirit.

Tuesday

Dear Lord and Master, who dost ever feed thy flock like a shepherd, keep us within thy fold this day and protect and guide us in all that we do.

Wednesday

Enable us, our Father, by the eating of this food, more courageously to face the battle of life and more faithfully to do thy will, whatever may be the sacrifices required of us.

Thursday

Eternal Father, thou hast given us an abundance of food for the nourishment of our bodies and hast given us Jesus so that by walking in his steps we may come unto thy holy throne. May we in his dear name eat this food and in his spirit live today.

Friday

Give us this day our daily bread, dear God, not only bread for our bodies but bread also for our minds and spirits. Make us to accomplish thy holy purposes for our lives in all that we do and all that we say.

Saturday

Holy Spirit of God, give thy blessing to each of us at this table, and may we love thee more fully, serve thee more faithfully, follow thee more loyally, and believe in thee more steadfastly.

TWENTY-SECOND WEEK

Sunday

Safely through another week, thou hast brought us on our way, providing food for our bodies and inspiration for our souls. Now, dear Lord, we rejoice that we may turn confidently toward tomorrow, assured of thy everlasting love and guidance.

Monday

O thou holy God who inhabitest eternity, we earnestly pray that thou wilt help each of us to contribute to the happiness of all with whom we are privileged to eat our daily meals.

Tuesday

Dear God, we know that it is a good thing to give thanks unto thee. May the measure of our thankfulness be equal to our determination to be obedient to thee in all that we undertake and do today.

Wednesday

Dear Father, help us to eat this meal in a spirit of joyful thanksgiving to thee for this food, for all whom we love and who love us, for health and strength, and especially for thy loving and continual presence.

Thursday

May the spirit of Christ be with us as we eat together in his name, and may the love of Christ fill our hearts with the peace which passeth all understanding.

Friday

With loving-kindness hast thou drawn us to thyself, heavenly Father, and we approach thee with prayers of thanksgiving for this food and all of the many expressions of thy beneficence.

Saturday

Whether we eat or drink, may we do everything to thy glory, from whom alone cometh every good and perfect gift.

TWENTY-THIRD WEEK

Sunday

Bless and guard, O Lord, each member of this household of faithful and true believers. Bless especially any who are now absent from our table. Protect and keep in thy love all whom we love. Support and encourage any who are lonely and despondent or grieving for the loss of friends and loved ones.

Monday

May our grocery bags, dear God, be filled not only with fruit and vegetables but also with appreciation and good will, and may this table be spread not only with an abundance of good food but also with cheerfulness, harmony, and thankfulness.

Tuesday

We thank thee, gracious Father, for those who in the preparation of this food have shown us an inspiring example of Christian living, and we pray that each of us may inspire others to love thee more perfectly.

Wednesday

Speak to each of us at this table, merciful God, in the still small voice which awakens, redeems, and revitalizes our minds and purposes according to thy holy will.

Thursday

Dear Jesus, who didst long ago break bread in love in the Upper Room, make this also an upper room where we feel thy presence and enjoy thy fellowship.

Friday

Forgive us, dear God, for being so slow to recognize and hesitant to acknowledge that this food and all of life's blessings come from thee, and quicken within us a lively sense of genuine gratitude.

Saturday

Even as we value food by its quality and not its quantity, so may we express our faith in thee not by loud boasting but by simple trust, sincere commitment, and quiet endeavor.

TWENTY-FOURTH WEEK

Sunday

If our spiritual testimony has been timid and our witness weak, Father in heaven, give us at this time new strength of body and nerve of soul so that we shall determine to be thy true disciples in the proclaiming of thy good news of salvation both today and throughout this week.

Monday

O most Holy Spirit, remove from our minds the blight of bitterness and from our souls the stain of sorrow, and keep us close to thy healing spirit as we eat this meal.

Tuesday

Give us, our Father, victory over all difficulties which encumber our growth as Christlike individuals. May we brighten the corners of our world by reflecting the light of thy countenance.

Wednesday

If by a thoughtless word or careless gesture we have brought heartache or suffering to anyone in our family or to any of thy children, we beseech thee to forgive us, dear God, and may we eat this food in the joy of a good conscience.

Thursday

Dear Lord and Savior Jesus Christ, we covet for our home the comforting words of assurance which thou didst speak after eating in the home of Zacchaeus: "This day is salvation come to this house."

Friday

Lord God, we bring to thee our broken promises and our unfulfilled dreams and pray that by love they may be mended and we renewed in our spiritual resolution even as this food gives us new physical vigor and energy.

Saturday

Gracious and forgiving Father, our prayer at this family meal is that the light of heaven may illumine our lives, our home, and our work today.

TWENTY-FIFTH WEEK

Sunday

God of our fathers, may we who sit together at this table be worthy of the heritage of faith bequeathed to us by our spiritual ancestors. May their good and faithful examples found within the pages of the Holy Bible and in the story of thy Church become a lamp unto our paths and a light unto our feet.

Monday

Heavenly Father, if we have attempted to quench our thirst from broken cisterns, lead us, we pray, to the Fountain of living water from which, if we drink, we shall never thirst again.

Tuesday

We worship thee in gratitude and praise, dear Father, for we know that every good and precious gift, including this food, comes from thy gracious and generous hand.

Wednesday

Keep us ever satisfied and grateful, O merciful Father, for all that thou hast given to us, and may we not be like the foolish man who in his greed for more than he needed tore down his barns and built greater barns but was neglectful of the welfare of his soul.

Thursday

Attune our hearts, dear God, to the joyous music of thy heavens, and may we with a cheerful melody of thankfulness partake of this food and go on our way rejoicing.

Friday

Lord of life and love, keep our hands and hearts united in Christian love at this family table, and help us to acknowledge our need for one another and for thee.

Saturday

Dear Jesus Christ, who didst promise thy rest and peace to all who labor and are heavy laden, comfort thy disciples gathered here in thy name that we may be restored in body and soul.

TWENTY-SIXTH WEEK

Sunday

On this Lord's Day when our thoughts center in the life and teachings of our Savior, bring to a lively flame within our souls a spirit of thankfulness, dear and loving God, that we may not eat this food in thanklessness or accept the loving labors of those who have provided these good gifts without appreciation.

Monday

Dear God, may we not fill our bodies and starve our souls, and may we who hunger and thirst for food and drink also hunger and thirst after righteousness.

Tuesday

We pray that thou wilt bless, Father in heaven, not only our family at this table, but also the family of man, our brothers and sisters in thee, whether they live in our neighborhood or far beyond the shores of our country.

Wednesday

Dear God, who didst provide manna for thy chosen people while they journeyed in the wilderness, we thank thee for providing bread to sustain and nourish us for our journey through this day.

Thursday

We praise and thank thee, eternal Father, for the many men who during many generations have cultivated new lands in this our beloved nation and planted fields from which come the bounties of this table.

Friday

Heavenly Father, may nothing which we say during this meal or do during this day separate us from thy love, and may our lives be made holy by the baptism of thy Holy Spirit.

Saturday

We thank thee, God of love, for this food and for every good gift which this day brings. Make us aware of the many ways by which we may employ this day to thy advantage and to the welfare of our souls.

TWENTY-SEVENTH WEEK

Sunday

Dear Lord and Master, in thy Holy Book we read the words, "O taste and see that the Lord is good: blessed is the man that trusteth in thee." May the taste of this food so remind us of thy providential love that by trusting in thee we too may receive thy blessing.

Monday

Grant thy blessing to each of us as we eat this meal, gracious Father, and may we find thee to be the shepherd of our souls and the guardian of our lives.

Tuesday

Dear God, we thank thee for such common products of field and farm as bread and milk and that by an uncommon and miraculous transformation they become energy and vitality providing health and strength for work and play.

Wednesday

Dear Lord, whose love is everlasting and whose mercies are greater than our need, we thankfully accept this food from thy hand and pray that we may serve thee as obedient children.

Thursday

Dear Jesus Christ, who didst take up a towel and wipe the feet of thy disciples and said that he who would be greatest should become as a servant, help us willingly and gladly to serve those with whom we eat this meal and all who may benefit by our services done in thy name.

Friday

Fortify our lives with food for our bodies and spiritual nourishment for our souls, heavenly Father, so that we may offer this day a courageous and adventurous testimony of our faith in thee.

Saturday

May this meal, dear God, be lit by the light of love, warmed by the flame of faith, and be made joyful by our thankfulness.

TWENTY-EIGHTH WEEK

Sunday

Our Father, may we ever worship thee in the beauty of holiness, and may our eating together on this day of peace and joy be made holy by thy presence among us and by our sincere gratitude for thy many blessings.

Monday

Even as thou didst speak, dear Jesus, of thy preoccupation with thy Father's business, so may we leave this table determined to do to the best of our ability the work which thou hast assigned to us.

Tuesday

Bless, dear God, all who today eat their bread in loneliness, and help us who enjoy the family fellowship of this meal to strive evermore to be Christlike in our love for all men.

Wednesday

Almighty God, may we who have found pleasure in eating food which sustains our physical life find an even greater joy in all that gives strength and vitality to our spiritual life.

Thursday

In everything and at all times and seasons we would give thanks to thee, O God, for thy gifts are greater than our reckoning, thy love beyond our deserving, and thy watchful protection without ending.

Friday

May we, thy children, find such strength through this nourishing food and through the reading of thy Word that we shall face this day and its responsibilities with heroic endeavor and aggressive good will.

Saturday

We thank thee, dear God, for this food and for the many joys which our family life provides.

TWENTY-NINTH WEEK

Sunday

Lord Jesus, who never looked upon any man as a stranger but welcomed everyone into the kingdom of love, may our door never be closed to those who come in need nor our table be too crowded to make room for loving friends who have been given to us by thee.

Monday

Bless not only this bread, holy Father, but bless also those whose labors have provided for us this food, and bless us with inner strength to do all that thou dost expect of us this day.

Tuesday

Dear God, bound by the ties of Christian love and devotion we join in thanksgiving unto thee from whom this food and all blessings continually flow.

Wednesday

Dear Father in heaven, help us to love one another more perfectly, and may everything we say and do at this table contribute to a happy family fellowship and to an increase in family love and loyalty.

Thursday

May this food contribute to the upbuilding of our bodies and the uplifting of our spirits, O blessed Lord, so that all we undertake today may honor and glorify thee, who art King eternal, immortal, invisible, the only wise God.

Friday

Grant us, dear Father, the wisdom and wit to perceive in the daily experiences of our lives, such as the breaking of bread, that everywhere there are miracles which we cannot fully comprehend with our minds but which by faith we may claim as our own possessions.

Saturday

Give nourishment at this time, loving Father, not only to our bodies by this food, but nourishment also to our hearts by our family love and nourishment to our souls by our common faith in thee.

THIRTIETH WEEK

Sunday

Dear Lord and Savior, whose love is beside us, above us, and within us, make us conscious as we partake of this food that thou art no less with us when we sit at this table as when we worship in church and no further from us when we break bread in love as when we kneel in prayer.

Monday

What can we offer unto thee, O Lord, for all thy benefits toward us? Such as we have we offer, even our contrite hearts, our joyous spirits, our prayers of thanksgiving, and our humble wish to walk ever with thee.

Tuesday

May we be thy good Samaritans, dear God, who cheerfully and generously share our food and worldly goods with all who have been hurt or neglected along the highways of life.

Wednesday

O thou who are clothed in glory and majesty, we pray that thy love may be our inspiration today, and may we, nourished by this food, become loyal children in thy kingdom of righteousness and peace.

Thursday

Heavenly Father, even as salt and spices add tone and taste to this food now set before us, so may our lives show kind and thoughtful words and a loving attitude toward one another.

Friday

Dear Lord, permit no unkind or thoughtless word to separate us from each other, and may we in peace and joy partake of this food which has been prepared for us by responsible and loving hands.

Saturday

Because our world needs warm friendship and tender compassion no less than food and drink, we pray, O loving God, that we may do our part to offer not only food to the hungry but also love to the lonely.

THIRTY-FIRST WEEK

Sunday

Dear God, may we whose salvation has been made secure by the cross of thine only Son consider all personalities, both those of our loved ones with whom we eat this meal and also those of strangers in far distant corners of the earth, to be of inestimable worth and pearls of great price.

Monday

Father in heaven, in a world which depends for food and shelter upon the labors of every man, may we cheerfully and earnestly do our part and not shirk from any task, however humble or trivial, that is given to us.

Tuesday

Dear Lord Jesus, may our table be like the one in Bethany where thou didst sit with Mary, Martha, and Lazarus, and may we, like them, find joy in thy companionship.

Wednesday

Give us, eternal Spirit, some worthwhile work to do this day, and be it difficult or easy, important or routine, give us strength of body and steadfastness of will to do it to thy glory.

Thursday

Even after we have finished this meal, dear God, and turn in various directions to work and play, may we not move beyond our common love for each other or beyond thy love for each of us.

Friday

May words of praise, dear Lord, be continually in our mouths, for though we are undeserving thou hast provided this food for our use and though we are unworthy thou hast looked upon us in mercy and in love.

Saturday

Dear Jesus, who hast taught us that whatever we ask the Father in thy name He will give, we who have received so much from his hand would not eat this food selfishly nor without concern for the great need of many of our human brethren.

THIRTY-SECOND WEEK

Sunday

God of all comfort, if we have come to this table with troubled minds and anxious hearts, may we remember the words of our Savior, "Come unto me, all ye that labor and are heavy laden, and I will give you rest." Give us on this day of reverent activity and quiet rest such preparation of mind and spirit as may be needed throughout this week.

Monday

Dear Shepherd of our souls, we, who cannot by ourselves provide even the food essential for our physical welfare, pray that thou wilt sustain us and provide that our need for spiritual adequacy may be met by the abundant sufficiency of thy grace.

Tuesday

Remove from us, our Father, the shabbiness of thanklessness, and adorn our spirits with the beautiful garments of a thankfulness that unceasingly finds joy in praising thee.

Wednesday

Most merciful God, may this food bring strength and health to our bodies, and may thy Holy Word bring light and guidance to our souls.

Thursday

Dear God, who granted us strength for yesterday's needs and hast promised to care for us tomorrow, we pray at this mealtime that thou wilt make this day one of spiritual adventure in companionship with thee.

Friday

Gracious and loving God, may this food and drink become visible tokens of an inner and spiritual gratitude to thee, for thou hast supplied all of our needs according to the fullness of thy inexhaustible love.

Saturday

Heavenly Father, stretch our minds, enlarge our hearts, and deepen our spiritual sensitivity so that we who have been given so much may not forget the plight of many who are undernourished and in want.

THIRTY-THIRD WEEK

Sunday

Dear Lord Jesus, may the touch of thy hand bring healing and comfort today to all who are brokenhearted and discouraged, and may we so vividly remember thy constant love that we shall eat this food in hope and joy. Give spiritual power to all thy servants who on this sacred day proclaim the coming of the Comforter to lonely and despondent people.

Monday

Because apart from thee our lives are without meaning, keep us, ever-loving God, close to thee as we eat this food and do not forsake us even when we forsake thee.

Tuesday

May thy gift of food, dear God, give us such strength and health that we may rise up on wings as eagles, run and not be weary, and walk and not faint.

Wednesday

Give us, eternal Father, the mind and heart of spiritual pioneers so that we shall bravely leave this table, determined to do and to dare in the building of thy kingdom of brotherhood and peace.

66

Thursday

Help us, our Father, to partake of this food reverently, for we know that rich soil is a manifestation of thy loving care, warm sunlight an evidence of thy providence, and all growing things a witness of thy holy purposes.

Friday

We are glad, holy Father, that in thy wisdom each of us has been created in a manner differing from every other person in the world, yet we pray that we may be one in our love for thee.

Saturday

May we not, dear God, so greatly desire foods that have not been provided that we fail to accept in gratitude the foods now prepared for our daily need.

THIRTY-FOURTH WEEK

Sunday

Dear Christ our Lord, on this and every Sunday we remember the promise and portent of thy glorious resurrection. In the name of thy living and abiding presence may we eat this food in joyous praise.

Monday

Help us, dear God, to enjoy the companionship of those with whom we eat this meal, and may we in love and patience add cheerfulness and encouragement to their lives.

Tuesday

We know, dear Jesus, that if we do not find thee at this table and in our home, we shall miss thee in the street, the business world, or school. We pray that we may ever be receptive to thy words and responsive to thy presence.

Wednesday

We bow our heads in prayer, O Lord, so that we may express our thankfulness and appreciation to thee for this life-invigorating blessing of good food.

Thursday

Heavenly Father, may our home and the loved ones with whom we eat this meal become an anchor which keeps us from drifting aimlessly through this day.

Friday

Dear God, may our faith in thee, our faith in thy Son, and our faith in the abiding presence of the Holy Spirit so free our troubled hearts that this mealtime may become a gateway to fullness of life.

Saturday

Fill our bodies, Lord of life, according to our physical need, but do not permit us to forget that those who truly hunger and thirst after righteousness shall receive from thee the joy of spiritual contentment.

THIRTY-FIFTH WEEK

Sunday

We thank thee, Father of mercies and Author of all good, for every instructive and inspiring word which our parents have offered in thy name. May we, like them, be ever mindful of the source from which flows all good gifts and the food which we now thankfully accept and eat.

Monday

When our efforts to build thy kingdom seem futile or of small consequence, help us to remember, dear Christ, that from the small seed comes the rich harvest of grain and that thou dost not measure success by goals reached but by conquests attempted in thy name.

Tuesday

Dear God, may we not too quickly or thoughtlessly consume this food which was not grown in a single night but only during a long growing season and through the labors of many persons.

Wednesday

Give us doubly of thy Spirit during this hour of family fellowship, dear God, that we may face faithfully and heroically the temptations and trials of life, and may we finally sit at the banquet table of thy Son in everlasting joy and peace.

Thursday
So inspire us with thy love, dear Father, that at this table we shall not only partake of this food but also enjoy the good will and pleasing conversation of those who are closer and dearer to us than any persons in the world.

Friday
We thy children look to thee, O God, for all that sustains and nurtures our bodies and souls. We humbly pray that we shall ever express our gratitude to thee by obedience and faithfulness.

Saturday
Infinite Father, who in love hast provided for us this food and hast taught us to love our neighbors as ourselves, help us always to seek our neighbors' good and in love to give preference to their needs, welfare, and happiness.

THIRTY-SIXTH WEEK

Sunday

Lord of the Sabbath, may we cherish no privilege which this day offers more highly than the opportunity to become better acquainted with thee. To thee we offer our thanksgiving for this food, for our loved ones, and for the days and joys of this new week.

Monday

If we have gathered together, heavenly Father, in sorrow or discouragement, may we remember that although we have exhausted our own resources, we cannot exhaust thy divine resources. In this knowledge may we now eat this food in thankfulness and praise to thee.

Tuesday

Open for us, dear God, a window toward Galilee that in reverence we may eat this food, always looking to him who dost offer words of eternal life, and inspired by his spirit, may we follow whithersoever he may lead today.

Wednesday

So kindle thy light upon the altar of our hearts, Holy Spirit, that we may ever pray faithfully and eat our meals thankfully.

Thursday

Dear Carpenter of Nazareth, give us thy blueprints for a better world, place thy tools within our hands, and may we find joy in building the foundations of thy kingdom. For this food and for the work to which thou hast called us, we give thee thanks.

Friday

May this our home, dear God, be none other than a house of God and the gateway to heaven. May this food prepare us to do more perfectly thy will.

Saturday

Most merciful Father, inscribe upon our hearts a genuine appreciation for this food and all of thy gifts, so that in times of trouble we may not be without blessed memories and a living hope.

THIRTY-SEVENTH WEEK

Sunday

That home is blest, dear Lord, where thou art loved the dearest, and that life is a blessing which, by emulating thy life, seeks to serve. Bless our home with thy love, and may we be a blessing to others. Bless this food to our use and us in thy service.

Monday

Help us, heavenly Father, not to ask from thee any blessings which by thy grace we do not ask for every other family in thy world.

Tuesday

O Lord God, our help in ages past and our hope for years to come, we pray that during this day we may sincerely love thee, enthusiastically serve thee, and worthily glorify thy name.

Wednesday

Empty our lives, God of all mercy, of all envy, bitterness, and smallness of mind and heart, and fill our lives with thy love and spirit as we eat this food in thy name.

Thursday

O God, who doth require of stewards that they be found faithful, we praise thy holy name for the great natural resources of soil and water from which comes this food on our table, and we pray that we may ever consider ourselves to be faithful stewards of all resources of land and sea.

Friday

Come down, Lord Jesus, by some secret stairway and enter into the life of each of us at this family table, so that whether we eat or drink, work or play, we may always seek to serve thee and thy kingdom.

Saturday

Thou who hast taught us that whatsoever a man soweth, that shall he also reap, help us to sow seeds of kindness, generosity, and gratitude. May we remember as we partake of this meal that he who soweth to the Spirit shall of the Spirit reap life everlasting.

THIRTY-EIGHTH WEEK

Sunday

O holy and ever-blessed God, we rejoice that we may be counted as members of thy worldwide Christian fellowship and participants in the activities and responsibilities of the Church universal. May this meal be for us a feast of Christian love, and may no words of ours discourage the communication of love among us.

Monday

Dear God, we who have seen thee in the face of Christ Jesus our Lord ask that his life may be so real in our lives that we shall always eat, work, and sleep according to his will.

Tuesday

O thou who didst create this world in which we live, we thank thee for the evidence in growing grain and ripening fruit that thou art evermore creating those things which give us life and health and strength.

Wednesday

O Master, let us walk with thee today. May we not turn from doing thy will. May we not be tempted to follow the easy road. May we ever strive to keep in step with thee. May we never forget that this food comes from thy loving hand.

Thursday

God of all comfort, who hast provided this food for our bodies and hast ever comforted us in our difficulties and tribulations, may we bring to all who are troubled the same comfort which thou hast given to us.

Friday

Give us, dear God, eyes not only to look thankfully upon this food but also eyes which discern invisible truths, and give us a proper focus so we may see all spiritual reality.

Saturday

Dear heavenly Father, may the beauty of Jesus so encompass and permeate our lives that through us thy gospel may be made attractive to those with whom we eat this meal and all others whose lives touch ours today.

Sunday

Set our feet upon the high road of spiritual quest today, Lord God. Help us to leave the shadows behind and to walk in thy light. May we not be satisfied or contented until we have done something worthy of our high calling in Jesus Christ our Lord. We thank thee for this food and for all ennobling visions of thy kingdom.

Monday

If we have forgotten thee, dear God, may we find in the constant love of those with whom we eat this meal a reminder of thy greater love for each of us.

Tuesday

If too long, heavenly Father, we have been spiritually nourished by the faith and testimonies of other men, give us such a personal confidence in thee that we may individually say, "My Lord and my God," and so eat this food in communion and fellowship with thee.

Wednesday

God our Father, a day is as a thousand years in thy sight and a thousand years as a day, but for us a day comes too quickly and passes all too soon away. We need thy guidance and instruction at this table and when abroad in the world, so that we may accomplish some worthy and useful task for thee.

Thursday

May the breaking of bread at this table be for us a sacred experience, heavenly Father and divine Lord, for thou hast set aside this food for the upbuilding of our bodies and the sustaining of our spirits.

Friday

We thank thee, dear God, not only for this food but also for the craftsmen who fashioned this furniture, designed tablecloth and napkins, and manufactured the dishes and silverware, and for all others who have contributed to the enjoyment of this meal.

Saturday

May we sense, Lord of all humanity, that this our table encircles in love the whole world, and we pray that thou wilt give us a true feeling of our brotherhood with all men of whatever creed or nation, for we all claim a common divine parentage.

FORTIETH WEEK

Sunday

On this Lord's Day we pray that every word we speak and every activity in which we engage, whether in church or at this family table, may be tested by the example of the Lord Jesus. May we always ask, "What would Jesus say or do?"

Monday

Dear God, make thy home with us and draw us close to thee as we thankfully partake of this food, and by thy providence may we one day find homelike thy temple not made with hands, eternal in the heavens.

Tuesday

Heavenly Father, may we who have received an abundance of food and so many other blessings from thy bountiful hand be numbered among the lamplighters along the paths that troubled and disheartened men must walk.

Wednesday

We acknowledge our many sins and transgressions, almighty God and everlasting Father, and we pray that at this table we may offer ourselves to the guidance of thy Holy Spirit.

Thursday

Dear Jesus Christ, who in love didst share the fellowship of many homes in Galilee long ago, we pray that thou wilt bless our home with thy presence as we eat this food in thy name.

Friday

Dear God, we thank thee that, sustained by the food set before us, we have been given the privilege of daily toil. Sanctify our work that it may not only contribute to our personal welfare but also serve the common good.

Saturday

O thou who keepest Israel and neither slumbereth nor sleepeth, help us during the hours of this day, both when we eat at this family table and when we turn to our various concerns and obligations, to magnify thy name and then in our rest at eventide to trust in thy watchful care.

FORTY-FIRST WEEK

Sunday

Dear Lord and Savior, may we continue today every good work undertaken yesterday, and begin today every good work we failed yesterday to undertake. For this food, for our mortal lives, and for the life of thy Spirit within us, we give thee thanks.

Monday

Dear God, we thank thee for the many lands from which have come the good things set upon our table and for the many people who have contributed to this meal.

Tuesday

Lord of all nations, may our Christian citizenship today be shown in our thankfulness to thee for home and food, in our loyalty to the high ideals and worthy endeavors of our fathers, and in our willingness to serve wherever there may be tasks for us to do.

Wednesday

Dear God our Shepherd, give to each of us who partake of this meal a vital sense of partnership with one another and with all who have responded to the high calling of Christ Jesus.

Thursday

May we endeavor this day, holy Father, to keep the unity of the Spirit in the bond of peace, and may everything we do at this table or away bring harmony within our home.

Friday

Let us remember, dear God, in gratitude that somewhere a farmer toils in a field, a miller labors, a sailor goes down to the sea by ship, and food is processed, transported, and marketed so that this and every home may have food each day.

Saturday

Dear God, whose glory the heavens declare, may we ever sing thy praises, for thou dost supply every worthy desire for which we crave: food, clothing, and shelter for our bodies, and ideals and heavenly goals for our minds.

FORTY-SECOND WEEK

Sunday

Eternal God, who hast spoken to us through parents, pastors, and teachers, may our eyes see and our ears hear all that by thy will encourages in us devotion to thee and loyalty to thy kingdom. Keep us steadfast in our faith in thee and always grateful for the food which thou hast provided.

Monday

Dear Lord and Savior, who calmed the waters of the Sea of Galilee and brought peace to the minds of thy disciples, be thou our stay and bring us again as a family to this table if it be thy will.

Tuesday

Into our empty hands, dear God, place food for our bodies, and into our waiting hearts put thy word of encouragement and peace.

Wednesday

May we recall with sincere devotion and remember with ardent thankfulness, dear Lord Jesus, the cross thou didst bear for the remission of our sins and that by thy sacrifice we are now enabled to eat this food at a table which is encircled by thy love.

Thursday

At this family table and among these persons whom we love more than life itself, we pray for the quiet benediction of thy Spirit, dear God, and for the abiding presence of thy Son.

Friday

May every day, infinite Father, bring us opportunities to reverence thy name through good works and to build thy kingdom through noble deeds. May we accept this food in the spirit of humble thankfulness.

Saturday

As we partake of this food, dear God, we pray that thou wilt bless all missionaries who in distant lands today feed the sick and teach thy words of everlasting life.

Sunday

Place a song in our hearts today, heavenly God. Where there is sadness may we bring joy, and where there is despair may we offer hope. So may this Sabbath Day bring thy peace to our hearts, and may we eat this food in gladness and gratitude.

Monday

Help us, divine Father, to do unto others as we would that they do unto us, to serve others as we would that they serve us, and to love others as we would be loved, and may we expect nothing from others that we are unwilling to give to them. May we eat this food not selfishly but gratefully.

Tuesday

Eternal Father, may the strength of thy everlasting hills be an inspiration for our weak lives, and may we who share this meal in thankfulness ever turn to thee for daily strength.

Wednesday

Dear God, who hast of old ordained that growth should come first in the blade, then in the ear, and finally in the full corn in the ear, help us who now eat together not to expect overnight to harvest the fruits of the Spirit, but rather by thy aid to labor continuously that we may finally produce in our lives the kind of Christian character thou dost expect and require.

Thursday

Awaken our awareness, O God, to the beautiful expressions of thy love and goodness to be seen in land, sea, and sky, to the reality of the inner world of the Spirit, and to these treasures of the earth which are now given for our nourishment.

Friday

Merciful Father, who hast brought us to thy kingdom for such a time as this, help us to understand that some things will never be done if we do not do them, and that by this food now set before us thou dost give us strength to do any task which thou hast given to us.

Saturday

Heavenly Father, if we have lived too long in the valleys of gloom, lift up our eyes unto the hills from whence cometh our help, and by thy Spirit make this daily meal a source for the renewal of our strength.

FORTY-FOURTH WEEK

Sunday

O Holy Spirit of God, bless our neighborhood and our community with thy love, and may we live in harmony, serve one another unselfishly, and come to know how good and how pleasant it is for brethren to dwell together in unity. May our home and this table where we break bread together animate the spirit of thy love.

Monday

Lord Jesus, who hast promised never to foresake us and hast now provided this food for our use, confirm once more our promise to serve thee and never to wander from thy pathway.

Tuesday

Heavenly Father, we thank thee for this food, and we pray that our words of thanksgiving may not be spoken so hurriedly that we do not wait to hear thee speak to us.

Wednesday

O God of light, if we walk this day in thy light, we shall have joyous fellowship with one another at this meal and with thy Son Jesus Christ.

Thursday

May we offer to thee our gratitude for this food, gracious God, in order thereby better to appreciate our benefits and to know that thy love passeth all understanding.

Friday

O thou divine Friend with whom by faith we keep company as we eat this food, we bless thee for our friends who comfort, encourage, and sustain us, and we pray that we, too, may be worthy of their friendship.

Saturday

Dear Jesus Christ, who hast taught us to seek first the Kingdom of God and his righteousness, help all in our family circle who sit together at this mealtime to give priority to those things which are of eternal value and to learn evermore to put first things first.

FORTY-FIFTH WEEK

Sunday

O God, bless thy Church universal and all who in fellowship with thee participate in thy work of sacrificial devotion. Grant that we may be willing to accept the blame for the world's turmoil and trouble, if in the darkness we have permitted our individual lamps of faith to become dim or to go out. Create in us such a spirit of thanksgiving for this food as shall sustain and support us throughout the days of this week.

Monday

As we gather at this family table, almighty Lord, make us conscious that we are members of a fellowship of saints that transcends all reckoning by time and place.

Tuesday

Heavenly Father, give to us who eat this food in recognition of thy sovereign goodness some new truth, challenge, or ideal from thy Holy Word which shall bring new life and hope into our lives today.

Wednesday

Teach us, divine Spirit, to discipline our desires, help us to be temperate in all things, and show us how through moderation we may preserve our health and thereby be enabled to serve thy kingdom more perfectly.

Thursday

O thou Giver of life, who hast provided this food for our use, fill our hearts with praise, and may we worship thee not only when morning gilds the skies but also when lengthening shadows darken the western horizon at eventide.

Friday

When our flesh is weak, Father almighty, and our will power falters, give us by thy Spirit a renewed commitment to serve thee, to live according to the light which thou hast provided, and at all times when we eat together to offer our thanksgiving in Christ's name.

Saturday

O God our Father, help us to brighten that corner of life in which thou hast placed us and to make cheerful and happy this hour at the family table.

FORTY-SIXTH WEEK

Sunday
Teach us, dear God, to be truly thankful. We too often take for granted the provision and the preparing of our daily bread. May we not leave this table before we first acknowledge our indebtedness to others and to thee.

Monday
May this meal, heavenly Father, satisfy more than our physical hunger. May it also bring us closer together as a family and give us a better understanding of each other and of thee.

Tuesday
Help us, our Father, as we partake of this food to be so sensitive to the needs of other people that we shall find ways of helping them without their asking, and may we do what we can without first calculating the cost or inconvenience to ourselves.

Wednesday
Dear God, permit no troubled thought to deprive us today of the beauties of this world, the blessings of our companionship at this family table, and the joy of knowing that thou art near us.

Thursday

May our prayers never become so habitual or our thanksgiving so routine, dear Lord, that we fail to perceive that with each new day come new blessings from thy hand.

Friday

Dear Jesus Christ, who didst come to seek and to save all who are lost, keep our feet from stumbling, direct us into paths of righteousness, and permit us to eat this meal in the knowledge that thy love is so broad as to embrace each of us.

Saturday

Dear God, we who have been called together in love to this family table pray that every word added and every deed recorded in thy Book of Life today may witness to our love for thee.

FORTY-SEVENTH WEEK

Sunday

Give us through worship today, Lord of the Sabbath, thy inspiration and guidance, and give us through this food the energy and strength to serve thee loyally until thy Son returns in glory.

Monday

We thy children pause at the beginning of this meal to offer our thanks, to acknowledge that thou art the Author of our lives, and to pray that thou wilt cast us in some useful role in the drama of human life today.

Tuesday

O Holy Spirit of God, who dost understand us more perfectly than we understand ourselves, help us more perfectly to thank thee as we partake of this food and to learn and then to do all which thou dost desire.

Wednesday

Dear God, in whom there is no darkness at all, guide our steps by thy holy light into the paths of joyous thanksgiving and family harmony.

Thursday

Father of mercies, who hath provided this food according to our need, help us to grow within our hearts flowers of generosity, gratitude, and grace.

Friday

Dear God, if after eating this meal we are called by thee to do battle for justice and righteousness, clothe us, we pray, with thy armor that we shall be able to stand and withstand any evil assault.

Saturday

May we learn, heavenly Father, to be joyful recipients of this food and of thy many gifts and not to be miserable or to complain because thou hast not given us everything we have asked for.

FORTY-EIGHTH WEEK

Sunday

Lord Jesus, bless all of thy servants who in obedience to thy great commission have left the warmth of their homes and family fellowship and are endeavoring in thy name to draw all men into thy kingdom. May those of us who eat in the security and quiet of this home recognize that we, too, must share in the work of thy kingdom.

Monday

O God, who didst place the distant stars and planets in their spheres and yet did not neglect to clothe the garden rose in indescribable beauty, we bless and thank thee for thy infinite concern for each of us and for thy provision for this food for the sustaining of our bodies.

Tuesday

Dear Lord Jesus, who art now and always the most welcomed Guest at every meal, may thy love be the loom upon which we weave the tapestry of our lives today.

Wednesday

Give us by thy grace, dear God, such self-mastery that we shall not permit carnal desire to overpower discipline, greed to replace gratitude, sin to deprive us of salvation, nor love of this world to close the gateway to thy spiritual world.

Thursday

Bless, heavenly Father, all who in thy name are gathered about this table, and we pray that the serenity, poise, and patience of thy dear Son may inspire us to holy living.

Friday

Dear God, who hast given us loved ones with whom to eat this meal and hast filled our cup to overflowing, fill our hearts also with an overflowing joy and cheerfulness.

Saturday

Eternal and ever-living God, by the baptism of thy Holy Spirit cleanse our lives this day, purify our motives, fulfill in us thy divine purposes, and make us aware that thou art always with us when we break bread in holiness.

FORTY-NINTH WEEK

Sunday

Dear God, may we who have been called by thy Son into the fellowship of the redeemed consider no man inferior or superior because his race or creed differs from ours. May we partake of this food in thankfulness for the whole family of man and for thee, who art the Father of all.

Monday

Compassionate Savior, rescue us from the sin of indifference toward the spiritual and physical needs of our brethren, and help us, insofar as we are able, to give of our substance, that by thy grace we may bring hope and health to other men.

Tuesday

Author of everlasting life, may we ever live together in a manner becoming to Christians, and may our home become for each of us a little heaven which radiates thy peace and joy.

Wednesday

O God, who dost give us food for the strengthening of our bodies, give us also the vision of new frontiers of the Spirit toward which we may move today with a dedicated and holy purpose.

Thursday

May we eat this meal, O Christ, within the lengthening shadows of thy cross, which is for us a sign of remembrance, challenge, conquest, and salvation.

Friday

Bless, dear God, each choice and decision we shall be required to make today, and may thy divine will be confirmed by the road we choose to follow.

Saturday

Give us, dear God, such a glowing thankfulness for this food and all of thy other blessings which enrich and support our lives that other men will wish to come to us to light their lamps.

FIFTIETH WEEK

Sunday

Holy and merciful God, may we show no disrespect toward any man for whom our Savior died. May we rather become channels of blessing by which all men may be drawn to thy throne of grace. May we praise and thank thee, not only in church on this Lord's Day, but also at this family table on each day of this week.

Monday

Help us who have been nourished by this food, heavenly Father, to fight today the good fight of faith, whereunto we have been called, that by thy grace we may lay hold of eternal life.

Tuesday

If life seems dull today, dear God, give us the enthusiasm of doing some new and adventurous thing for the upbuilding of thy kingdom.

Wednesday

Dear Lord and Master, we have left the doors of our hearts ajar today, and we pray that thou mayest enter and reside with us, bringing happiness to our home and peace to this table where we partake of bread and meat in thy name.

Thursday

Heavenly Father, in the name of Christ Jesus, who didst pray that thy will, not his, be done and hast taught us always to thank thee for our daily bread, cleanse our hearts of every selfish thought or self-seeking gain, so that our lives may no longer be self-centered but rather Christ-centered.

Friday

May thy glorious rainbow, ever reminding us of thy covenant of love, protection, and peace, always be above our table and our home, dear heavenly Father.

Saturday

In thee, gracious God, do we put our trust, by thy love we have been given this food for our happiness and health, and for thy kingdom we would offer our talents and efforts today.

FIFTY-FIRST WEEK

Sunday

Dear Lord of heaven and earth, who hast given us Sunday for rest and relaxation, help us worthily to use this day for the upbuilding of our spiritual lives, for the strengthening of the ties of love with each other and with thee, and for thanksgiving to thee for thy many blessings including this food which we eat in thy name.

Monday

Dear Father, may we hunger and thirst for both this food and drink which thou hast given for our use and also for that spiritual bread and living water with which Christ our Lord satisfies the deeper longings of our souls.

Tuesday

Enkindle in our hearts a warm flame of appreciation to thee, dear God, for thy provision of room and board, and may we always express our gratitude by love and loyalty to thy kingdom.

Wednesday

Give us grace, O God, to worship thee not only with our voices in church on Sunday but also by the work of our hands at midweek. Cause us now with thankfulness to accept this food so that we may be strengthened in our determination to be thy obedient servants.

Thursday

Help us, merciful God, to be willing to share thy manifold blessings with our fellow men who need food, clothing, and shelter.

Friday

As we look in gratitude upon this food set before us, make us aware, heavenly Father, of the invisible world in which thou dwellest and toward which thou dost call our spirits.

Saturday

Eternal Spirit, Source of light and life, give us pure minds and strong hearts to accomplish those purposes which thou hast for each of us. May this food become a means whereby we may more eagerly and more perfectly do justly, love mercy, and walk humbly with thee.

FIFTY-SECOND WEEK

Sunday
Bless, dear God, our home, our family, and our friends, and give us Sabbath rest and peace as we partake of this food in thy name and enjoy Christian fellowship in thy spirit.

Monday
We thank thee, gracious and good God, for field and forest, for rivers and oceans, for rich soil and waving grain, and for every way by which the world of nature provides those things needed for our health and happiness.

Tuesday
O thou who art our Father, increase and multiply our thanksgiving, and may we receive with heartfelt praise thy gift of food for which we are indebted to farmers, bakers, merchants, and particularly to thee.

Wednesday
O God, who dwells both in highest heaven and also within the hearts of faithful men, in thy presence are pleasures forevermore. Stir up within us such thankful joy that we may eat this food in a spirit of cheerfulness and with gladness of heart.

Thursday

O God of peace, teach us that in quietness and in confidence we shall find daily strength. Bless this food and bless us also as we hopefully and earnestly undertake whatever work thou hast assigned to us.

Friday

O thou who didst walk the garden paths in Eden in the cool of the day, come, we pray thee, into our home, be present as we eat this food, and abide with us in all of our labors.

Saturday

Dear God, who openest thy hand and satisfiest the desire of every living creature, thou hast been good to us beyond our need and reckoning. Create in us a corresponding thankfulness, and may we accept this food with praise and gratitude.

TABLE GRACES
FOR
SPECIAL DAYS
AND
OCCASIONS

TABLE GRACES FOR SPECIAL DAYS
AND OCCASIONS

For Birthdays

O God, who hast given us the priceless gift of life and hast provided this food for our nourishment, we thank thee for our loved one whose birthday we joyously celebrate today. So bless [*name*] that *he* may find happiness in thy service and contentment in every tie which binds *his* heart to ours in Christian love.

For Anniversaries

As we partake of this food today, dear Lord, we are mindful of the many ways by which thy love has guided us on our journey through life. We are especially thankful for this red-letter day, its beautiful memories of the past, and its bright anticipations for tomorrow.

In Sickness

Dear Lord and Savior, who didst in love heal the sick and restore them to their families, may thy blessing be with [*name*] who today is sick and unable to be·in *his* place at our table. May food and rest give strength, may medicine give healing, and may our love comfort and encourage *him*.

In Sorrow

Thou hast promised, dear Jesus, that they that mourn shall be comforted, and we in faith claim thy promise for all who sit at this family table. Give us the knowledge that thou art very close to us. Give us courage and confidence. Ease our heartache, but do not take from us the precious memories and cherished thoughts of [*name*] whom we have loved and lost until that day when by thy providence we shall be reunited forevermore.

When Guests Are Present

We bless and thank thee, dear God, that these friends are welcomed to our family circle today. May our understanding, appreciation, and love for one another grow in grace, deepen in meaning, and become a rich blessing as we break this bread in thy holy name.

When Leaving Home

O thou whose love, guidance, and protection are broader than the measure of man's mind, give thy blessing to [*name*] who today leaves our family table. Be with *him* in all *he* undertakes, sustain *him* with thy love, and may *he* return safely once again to those who will always be with *him* in love and spirit.

When Traveling

Give to us, eternal God, thy companionship as we travel today. May we come to appreciate the joys of the open road and this wonderful world which thou hast created for our pleasure. Bless this food that we in turn may bless thee wherever we may be.

New Year's Day

O thou who art the Lord of life, we thank thee that thou hast brought us to the threshold of a new year. Increase our faith according to our needs. May we wholeheartedly and cheerfully accept the responsibilities, enjoy the privileges, and appreciate the opportunities that another year offers. We pray that thou wilt provide not only food for our bodies but also lofty and inspiring visions for our souls.

Lent

Dear Father, may this season of remembrance of the life and sacrifice of our Savior bring to us a new sense of purpose for our lives and a quickened endeavor to know and to do what he requires of us. May we eat this food in the knowledge that every good and perfect gift comes from thy hand.

Palm Sunday

Heavenly Father, if any at this table have become spiritually complacent, may we by the remembrance of our Lord, who set his face steadfastly toward Jerusalem, learn that there is a road of loyalty, service, and sacrifice which calls each of us to our Jerusalem.

Easter

On this day of joy and gladness, we rejoice, dear God, that thou didst bring forth from the tomb thy Son and that he is our living Lord, who is always near us and ever our Companion and Friend. May his radiant spirit be with us as we eat this meal in his name and for his glory.

Mother's Day

We accept with grateful hearts, loving God, this food which thou hast provided and thank thee for the loving mother's hands which hast prepared it. We bless thee for our home and family, and especially do we thank thee today for our mother whose wise and gentle and patient love has made this a happy and beautiful home.

Father's Day

Dear God and Father of mankind, we thank thee for all fathers in whose lives are reflected thy loving care and concern for our physical and spiritual welfare. For our own father whose initiative and labor have given us food and shelter and safety, we give thee thanks. We pray that we may be found worthy of all he has done for us.

Thanksgiving Day

O thou eternal Source of life, we humbly thank thee that thou didst lead our fathers to this goodly land which indeed floweth with milk and honey and whose rich soil sustains our lives with food and freedom. Bless our native land, her fertile fields, her towering factories, her churches, schools, and homes. May we ever be thy holy people and brothers to all mankind.

Christmas

Dear Christ, who long ago was born in a stable because there was no room in the crowded inn, may we prepare a place for thee at our table and make room for thy spirit within our hearts. May the Christmas star so guide us that we shall find the abundant life which thou dost give to all who love thee.

TABLE GRACES
FOR
CHILDREN

TABLE GRACES FOR CHILDREN

I

Dear God, may we always be thankful for thy good gifts, for food and home and those whom we love.

II

Bless each one of us, dear God, and may we eat this food with thankfulness to thee, who art the giver of every good and perfect gift.

III

Dear Jesus, come into our home, be with us at our table, and give to each of us thankfulness for this food and all of thy many blessings.

IV

Heavenly Father, help us to love each other and to show our love by being kind and thoughtful and thankful.

V

Dear Father in heaven, may we who have good food, warm clothing, and a home which shelters us from wind and rain always remember to pray for children who do not have these things.

VI

Dear God, we are truly thankful to thee for giving us this food, and we pray that it may bring us health and strength.

VII

Dear God, we thank thee for everyone who has helped to provide this food for our use and especially for farmers in the fields, laborers in factories, and those who have worked in kitchens.

Charles L. Wallis is a skilled and experienced writer and editor, who has compiled many anthologies of an inspirational nature. He is minister of the Keuka College Church, New York, and chairman of the Keuka College Department of English. Among his anthologies are SPEAKERS' ILLUSTRATIONS FOR SPECIAL DAYS; A TREASURY OF POEMS FOR WORSHIP AND DEVOTION; WHEN CHRISTMAS CAME TO BETHLEHEM; THE TREASURE CHEST; and THE ETERNAL LIGHT.